Guitar Tunings

WISE PUBLICATIONS
London / New York / Paris / Sydney / Copenhagen / Madrid

Exclusive Distributors:
MUSIC SALES LIMITED
8/9 Frith Street, London W1V 5TZ,
England.
MUSIC SALES PTY LIMITED
120 Rothschild Avenue, Rosebery, NSW 2018,
Australia.
MUSIC SALES CORPORATION
257 Park Avenue South, New York, NY 10010,
United States of America.

Order No. AM954272
ISBN 0-7119-7234-6
This book © Copyright 1998 by Wise Publications.

Written by Joe Bennett.
Book design and layout by Digital Music Art.
Cover design by Michael Bell Design.
Cover and text photographs by George Taylor.
Artist photographs courtesy of LFI.
Printed in the United Kingdom by
Caligraving Limited, Thetford, Norfolk.

Your Guarantee of Quality:
As publishers, we strive to produce
every book to the highest commercial standards.
The music has been freshly engraved and
the book has been carefully designed to
minimise awkward page turns and to
make playing from it a real pleasure.
Particular care has been given to specifying
acid-free, neutral-sized paper made from pulps
which have not been elemental chlorine bleached.
This pulp is from farmed sustainable
forests and was produced with special
regard for the environment.
Throughout, the printing and binding have
been planned to ensure a sturdy, attractive
publication which should give years of enjoyment.
If your copy fails to meet our high standards,
please inform us and we will gladly replace it.

Music Sales' complete catalogue describes
thousands of titles and is available in
full colour sections by subject, direct from
Music Sales Limited.
Please state your areas of interest and send a
cheque/postal order for £1.50 for postage to:
Music Sales Limited, Newmarket Road,
Bury St. Edmunds, Suffolk IP33 3YB.

Visit the Internet Music Shop at
http://www.musicsales.co.uk

Wen most of us pick up a guitar for the first time, we take it for granted that there is a correct way to tune the instrument. But there's no real reason that we always have to use EADGBE just because it's the first tuning we learn. Players have been detuning and retuning their guitars since the birth of the blues in the early part of this century. Indeed, if you go back far enough, even the guitar's 16th-century ancestors used altered tunings – the lute and viluela, for example, were often tuned GCFADG.

And there is no shortage of contemporary players using tunings. A simple half-step drop (i.e. detuning the whole guitar by a semitone) was often favoured by rock and blues players like Jimi Hendrix, Kurt Cobain, Stevie Ray Vaughan and Nuno Bettencourt. At the other extreme, there are many totally unrelated tunings, as used by acoustic players like Crosby, Stills & Nash, Davey Graham and Joni Mitchell, or heavy metal acts like Korn.

Guitar Tunings To Go ! gives you an introduction to the most commonly-used tunings, and provides examples of how they can be used, with chord shapes for each new tuning. Once you've attempted these, try tweaking strings here and there to create new possibilities. You may even invent a tuning that no-one's ever heard of before. And if you do, make sure it goes in the next edition of this book!

Tuning tips

- Many tunings require the pitch of the string to be altered quite drastically. This can lead to broken strings (when the pitch is raised too far) or fret-buzz and poor tone (when lowered too far). For this reason, you may find that a new tuning requires a different set of strings. As a rule of thumb, if you have to alter a string's pitch by more than a whole tone (i.e. two frets' worth), you should really think about a different string gauge if you're going to use that tuning regularly.

- All the tunings in the book are shown relative to standard tuning (see right). However, you'll find it much easier to quickly and accurately retune a string if you use a chromatic electronic guitar tuner. These start from around £15.

- Some tunings will require a change in your technique in order to get the best out of them. Open chord tunings (e.g. 'Open D') generally sound good with big, wide strums, but some more unusual ones (e.g. 'All The 4ths') can be more effective with single notes or even harmonics. Of course, this can be a good thing too – a new tuning is a great way to get your playing out of bad habits.

- If you're an electric player, it is recommended that you try these tunings on a guitar which does not feature a floating bridge/locking trem system. Their fulcrum design makes tuning shifts time-consuming and inaccurate.

- If you're going to explore open chord tunings, you really should consider buying a bottleneck or 'slide'. They cost from £3-£10.

Tunings

Shown in the middle row of each chart are the note-names of the strings.

The top row represents the string numbers (the 6th string is the thickest on a regular guitar.)

6	5	4	3	2	1
D	G	D	G	B	D
-2	-2	0	0	0	-2

The numbers below show how much the string has to be raised or lowered in relation to normal EADGBE tuning.

Fretboxes

Fretboxes show the guitar upright *i.e.* with the headstock, nut and tuning pegs at the top of the picture – six vertical lines represent the strings.

The x symbol means you should not play this string

The o symbol means play the string 'open' without fretting a note

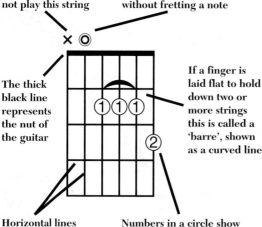

The thick black line represents the nut of the guitar

If a finger is laid flat to hold down two or more strings this is called a 'barre', shown as a curved line

Horizontal lines represent the frets, vertical lines the strings

Numbers in a circle show which finger you should use to fret the note

Chord notation

Chord tab is drawn with the guitar on its side, with the thickest string at the bottom – six horizontal lines represent the strings.

The top stave shows the chord as it would appear in traditional music notation

Below is the tablature – the numbers represent the fret positions. A zero means the string should be played open

Neil Young and his fellow country rockers, Crosby, Stills & Nash were responsible for some of the most extreme tunings of the 1960s.

1

Dropped D Tuning

6	5	4	3	2	1
D	A	D	G	B	E
-2	0	0	0	0	0

The simplest way to retune a guitar is to alter the pitch of the sixth string – these are referred to as 'dropped' tunings. Of these, the most useful is dropped D. Its most common usage is when you're playing in the key of D, because it produces a deep, resonant six-string chord from an ordinary D shape (see below).

Because only one string is altered from regular tuning, some of the open chords you already know won't have to change to suit the tuning; for example, C, Am, B7 and Dm are all the same shapes, but the Dm can also feature the two bass strings.

The low D bass note also provides new riff possibilities; you'll find that you can create rock riffs just by flattening your finger over the three bass strings and moving it around.

Famous users of dropped D include The Beatles, Manic Street Preachers, John Denver and James Taylor.

Tuning Guide

To get to dropped D from normal EADGBE tuning, you need to make sure the sixth string sounds exactly one octave lower than the fourth string. To do this, play the fourth string open (if you were in tune to start with, this will be a note of D) and gradually turn the sixth string's peg until the note sounds the same (some guitarists like to play a 12th fret harmonic on the sixth string for greater accuracy). As a final check, play an open D chord and strum all six strings.

D

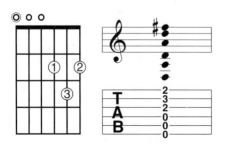

E

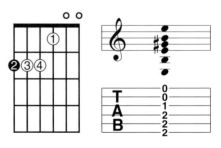

Guitar Tunings To Go!

Basic chords

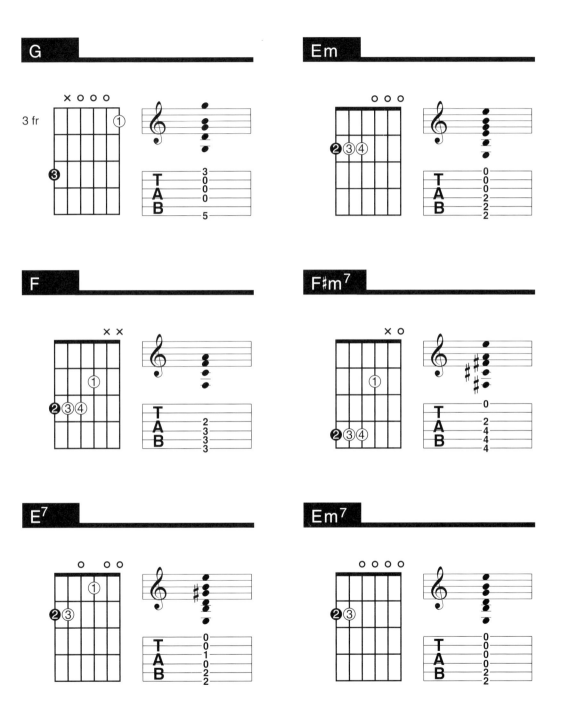

Because of the dropped bass note, any chords which had their root note on the sixth string in normal tuning will now have to be refingered. These are some of the most common versions.

D chords

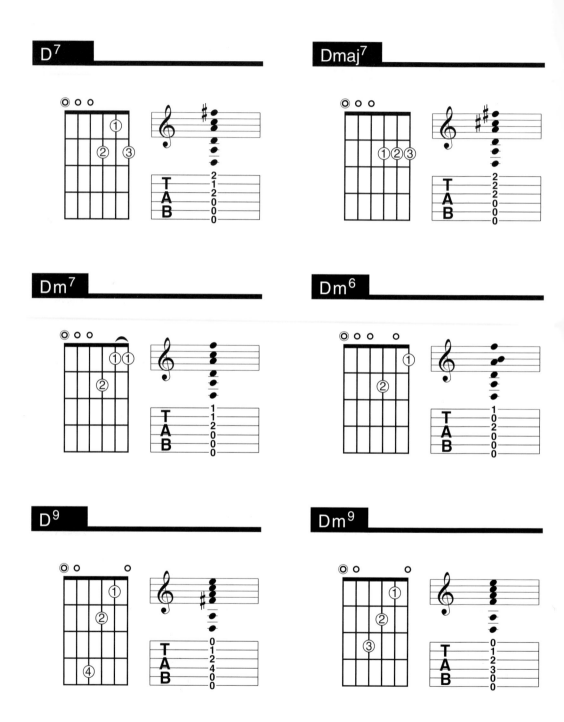

The compromises you have to make for some chords (see previous page) are more than worth it when you hear the great sounds that can be produced with that deep bassnote. All of these chords use six strings.

Further ideas

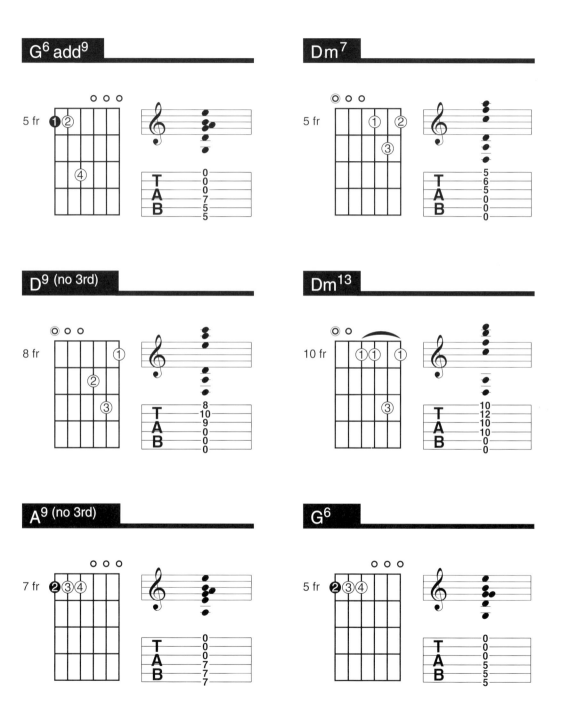

By using higher fret positions in conjunction with with altered sixth string, the above exotic-sounding chords can be created. Despite the jazzy names, these shapes are just as useful in rock and folk styles.

'Gimme 5'

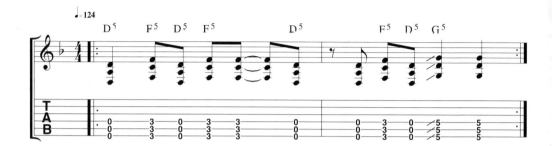

The dropped D bass note can be used to create very simple one-finger power chords. This example uses the open position, plus the 3rd and 5th frets, but you could also try the 7th, 10th and 12th fret versions when you're trying out your own ideas. This type of riff can sound like the Rolling Stones or Pantera, depending on how much distortion you use!

'Come Out To Play'

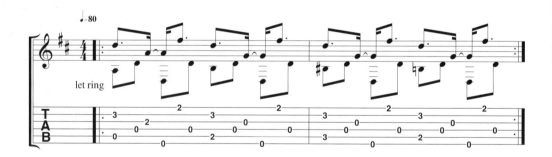

That resonant sixth string can also work well if used as a drone note in a fingerstyle part. This example features the thumb playing an alternating bass line on the fourth, fifth and sixth strings, with one finger each picking the first, second and third strings. The co-ordination can be difficult at first, so start slowly and gradually build up speed.

George Harrison learned fingerstyle guitar – and the Dropped D tuning – from Donovan.

Double Dropped D Tuning

6	5	4	3	2	1
D	A	D	G	B	D
-2	0	0	0	0	-2

If you can drop the sixth string from its usual pitch of E to D, it stands to reason that you can do the same with the first string. Although this tuning isn't as common as dropped D, the possibilities it provides make it well worth a look, especially if you're interested in songwriting.

In this chapter are some fingerings you can use to create straightforward open chords, but as with most tunings, more interesting effects can be created when you play chords that are impossible in regular tuning. Try playing a normal C chord shape then taking your first finger off while you strum five strings. The resulting open Cmaj9 sound can't be reproduced in any other tuning.

The dropped first string is most useful in this tuning when played open, so try other normal open chord shapes (e.g. C, Am, Em) to hear how that open first string changes the sound.

Tuning Guide

Once you've got the sixth string detuned to D (see previous chapter), you need to lower the first string by a whole tone (two frets' worth). The first, and easiest way to do this is to fret the second string at the third fret, then lower the pitch of the first string until it matches the fretted note (there should be no discernible 'wobble' when both notes are played together). A slightly more accurate method is to play a harmonic at the 12th fret of the fourth string, and tune the first string to that.

D

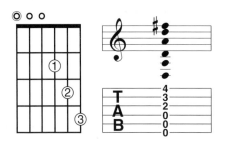

E

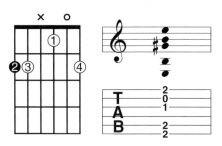

Basic chords

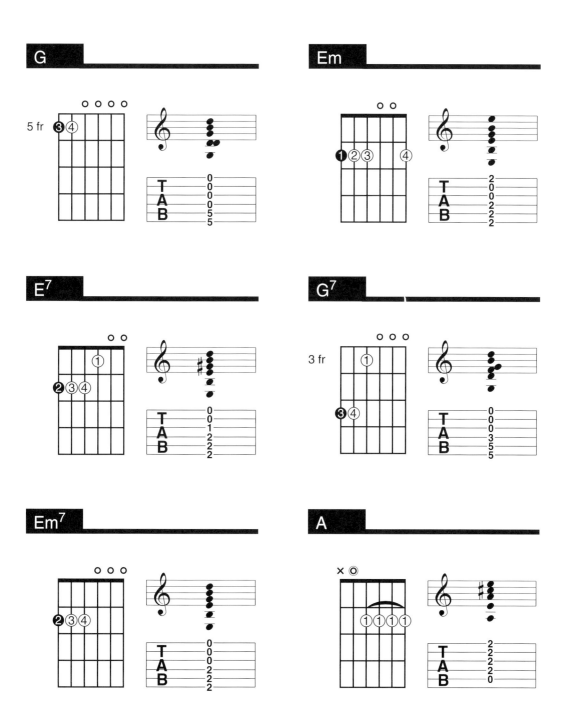

Most of these chords sound similar to their regular-tuned counterparts, but there are subtle differences. The G7 and Em7 are richer-sounding, and the open A has the added advantage of being dead easy to play!

D chords

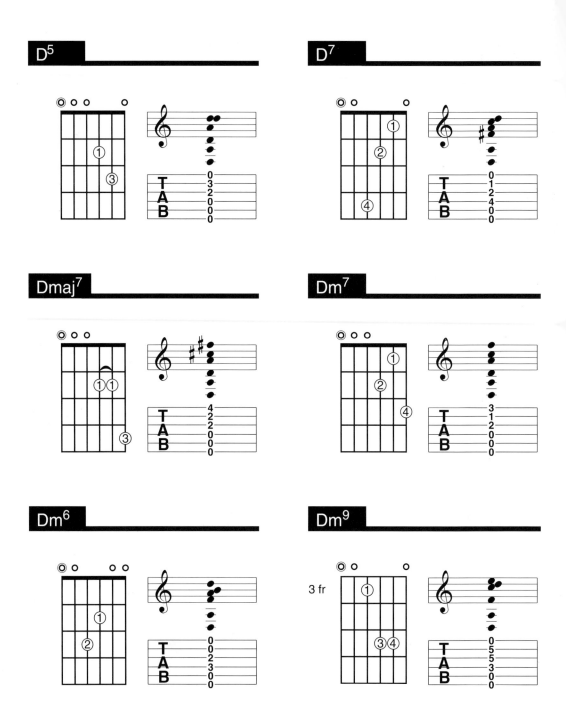

Here are six examples which have the sixth string D note as their root. The Dm9 uses the open string to create a cluster of three consecutive notes – great for arpeggios. Note the doubled note in the D5 chord.

Further ideas

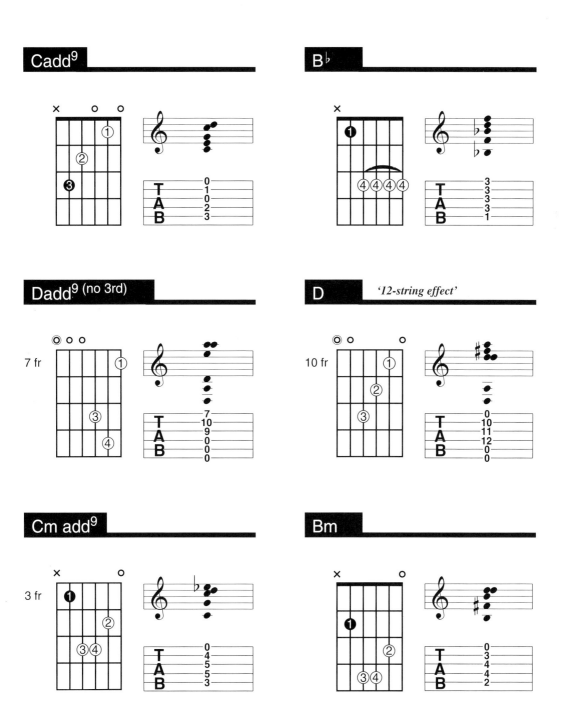

Shown here are some other chords which use the open top D as an added note, plus three which use doubled notes. The 12-string effect is created using a combination of octaves and unison notes.

'AK-47'

Picking across an open chord while letting the notes ring on is a useful technique in normal tuning, but when you're in an altered tuning the results can be beautiful. This two-chord example uses the open D note to create a slight clash with the fretted chord notes. Don't be put off by the difficult sounding chord name in bar 2 – the shape itself is fairly easy.

'Widdly Diddly'

This folk-style acoustic riff makes full use of the tuning – bass note, open-note pull-offs, unisons, even a harmonic. The example suggests letting the bass note ring on throughout the bar, but it can be shorter, or even omitted entirely if you wish. As with much fingerstyle folk guitar, there are bonus points for being able to play it at a ridiculous speed!

3

Open G Tuning

6	5	4	3	2	1
D	G	D	G	B	D
-2	-2	0	0	0	-2

This is the first open tuning we've looked at – that is, it creates a simple chord when you strum all the strings. This gives the player the advantage of being able to create any major chord simply by barring the first finger across all the strings (see below).

Some blues players refer to open G as 'Spanish' tuning, and more recently it has even been called 'Keef' tuning, because The Rolling Stones' Keith Richards uses it (albeit removing the sixth string from his guitar). However, it's also been under the fingers of folk players such as Joni Mitchell or John Renbourn, as well as bluesmen like Robert Johnson and Muddy Waters.

Like all open chord tunings, open G is used extensively by slide players. If you try the tuning using bottleneck, experiment with single-note and double-stopped licks as well as full chords – you may surprised how easily you can achieve classic blues effects!

Tuning Guide

To produce open G from regular tuning, drop the first and sixth strings to a pitch of D (see the previous chapter) to produce Double Dropped D tuning, then play the (now dropped) sixth string at the fifth fret. Drop the fifth string until its pitch matches that of the fretted note. Alternatively, play a harmonic on the 12th fret of the fifth string, and keep lowering its pitch until it matches that of the open third string. To check if you're in tune, just strum all the strings at once!

G

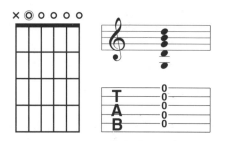

C

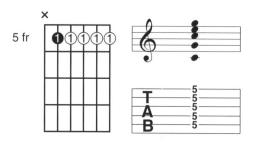

Basic chords

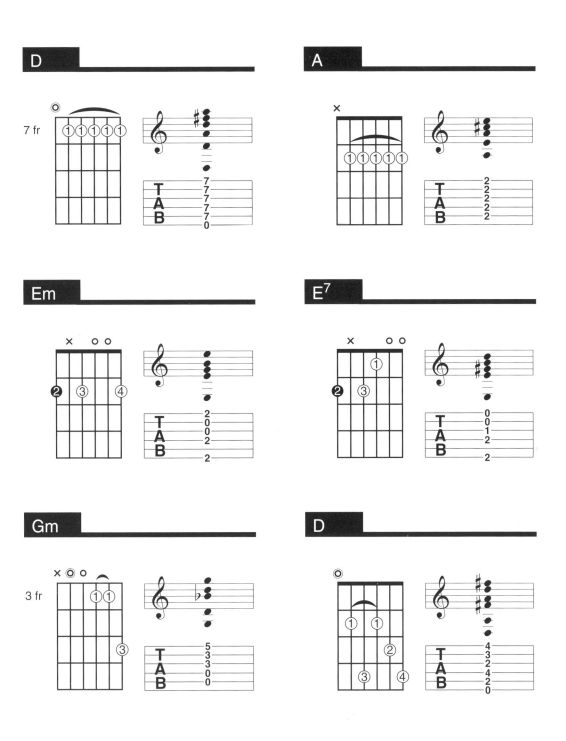

Once you've tried a few straight barre shapes (open G, C, D and A shown), try the more difficult seventh and minor examples here. I've also included the awkward but extremely useful 2nd fret version of D.

G chords

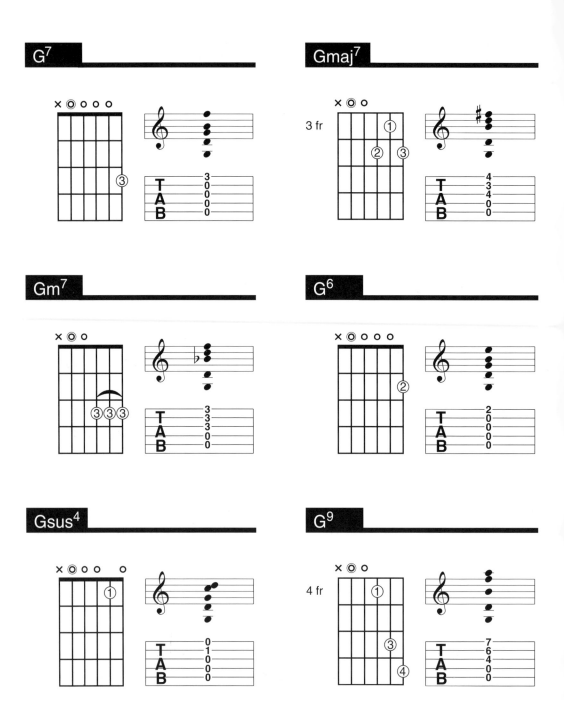

Because the tuning does so much of the work for you, most of the chords which have a root note of G are very easy to play. There are dozens more variations, many of which use only one finger.

Further ideas

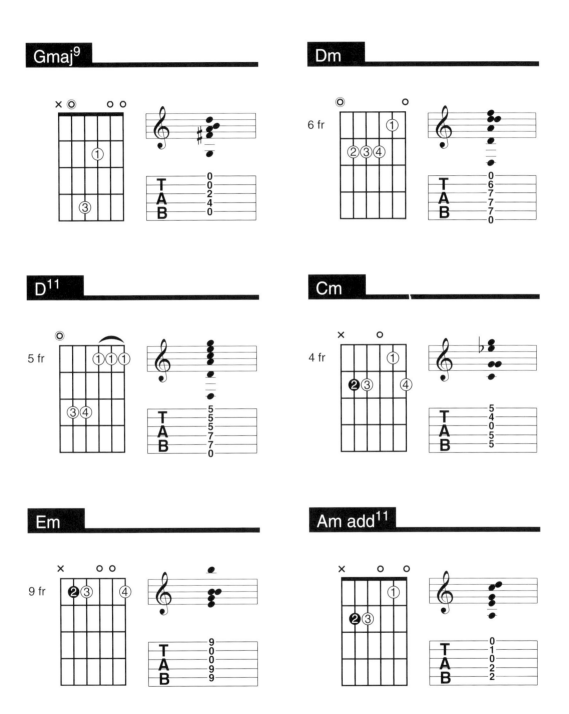

The price you have to pay for the convenience and sound of those G chords is that other shapes can be very difficult to work out. Here are some of the more unexpected shapes that the tuning allows.

Further ideas

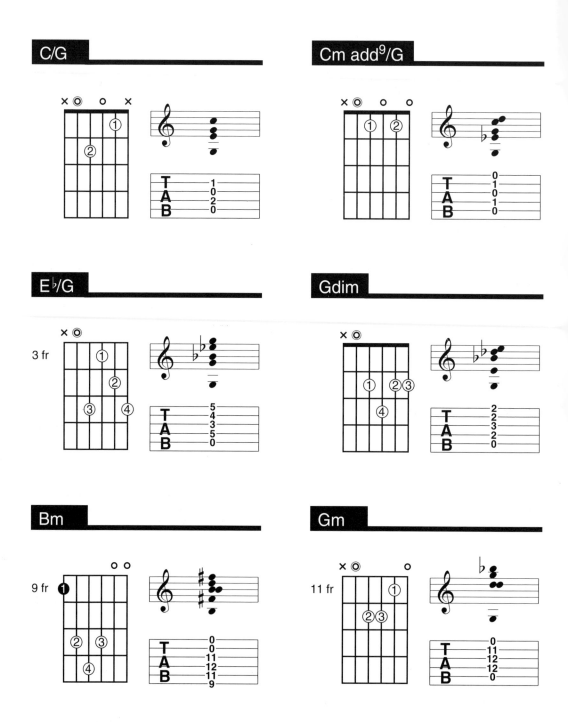

Another use of altered bass notes is to create 'slash chords', where the chord and bass note are different. I've shown three examples, plus some other chords which you may find useful in the key of G.

'Woke Up This Mornin'

If you're new to bottleneck techniques, this simple blues riff is a great place to start. It demonstrates four slide techniques in the open G tuning – chord playing, double-stops, a single-note lick and vibrato. This type of lick is typical of Robert Johnson, and works equally well if, like him, you try it with a capo. Remember that the slide should be over, not between, the frets shown.

'Demerara Rock'

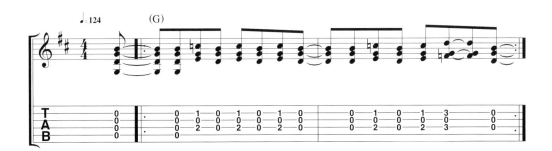

With the open 5th string acting as a drone note, you can alter the chords in rhythm to create some great riffs – Keith Richards has built a career on this idea! This example is typical of his style, and doesn't make any use of the two outer strings. Use up- and down-strokes, and don't worry too much about accuracy – it's fine if the open notes ring on a little longer than shown.

'Love Struck'

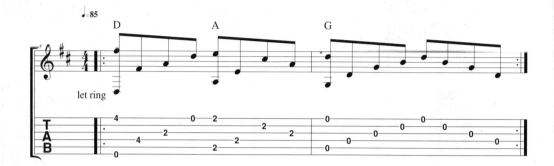

Once you've mastered the difficult D chord shape, the A and G chords here are a barre and an open chord respectively. You'll get the smoothest flow of notes if you use your thumb for the fifth and fourth strings, and three fingers for the first three strings. These techniques and shapes were used (with a capo) by Mark Knopfler in Dire Straits' *Romeo And Juliet*.

'Frantic Folk'

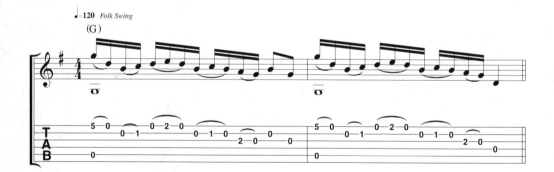

Once you start to let your playing work with the tuning, you'll find there are many technical advantages to playing in open G. This example features the ringing G bass note, while making maximum use of the hammer-ons and pull-offs available. If you can get your technique rhythmically accurate, you should be able to play this even faster than the ♩=120 shown.

4

Open D Tuning

6	5	4	3	2	1
D	A	D	F#	A	D
-2	0	0	-1	-2	-2

Open D is the deepest-sounding of the commonly-used open tunings. As a bottleneck tuning, it's the second most popular after open G. It's one of the few altered tunings to create a six-string major chord when strummed open, and this is perhaps why it has several variants – the two most common being open C (the whole tuning dropped a whole step) and open E (raised a whole step). Bear in mind that if you opt for open E, you'll have to raise the pitch of the fifth, fourth and third strings, increase the risk of breakage. You might be better sticking with open D and using a 2nd fret capo if you want to play in the key of E.

Artists who have used the tuning include Joni Mitchell (who used it with a capo), Leo Kottke (who detuned it into lower registers), Eric Clapton and Pearl Jam.

Tuning Guide

Drop both the outer two strings down to D (see the first two chapters), then fret the fourth string at the fourth fret, creating a note of F#. Lower the pitch of the open third string until it matches exactly. Now play the (lowered) third string at the *3rd* fret, and lower the pitch of the second until it's the same. To check the second string, play it against a 12th fret harmonic of the 5th string – both should sound the same. Strum the full six-string open chord to check the D chord is in tune.

D

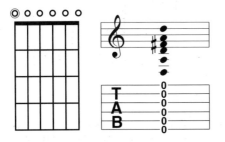

G

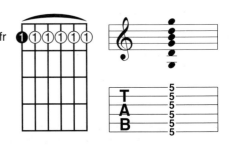

Basic chords

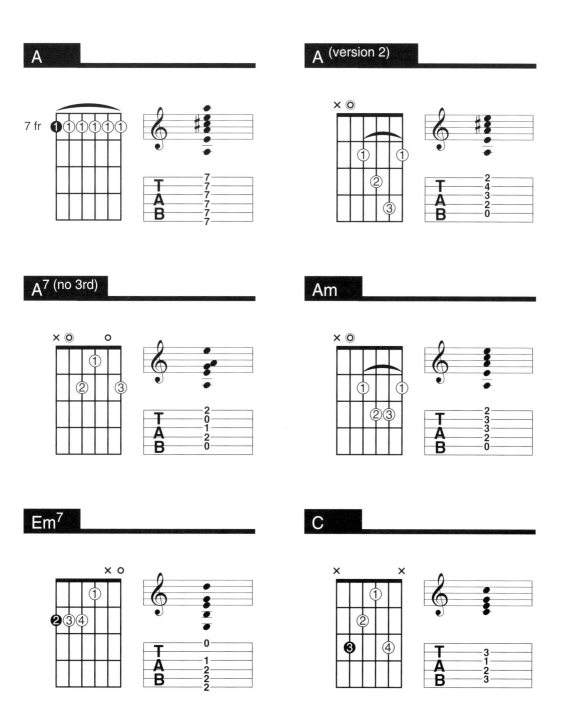

Due to the A bass note on the fifth string, chords with a root of A are as easy as some of the D chords available in this tuning. Some chords, like the Em7 and C shown here, require careful use of muting.

D chords

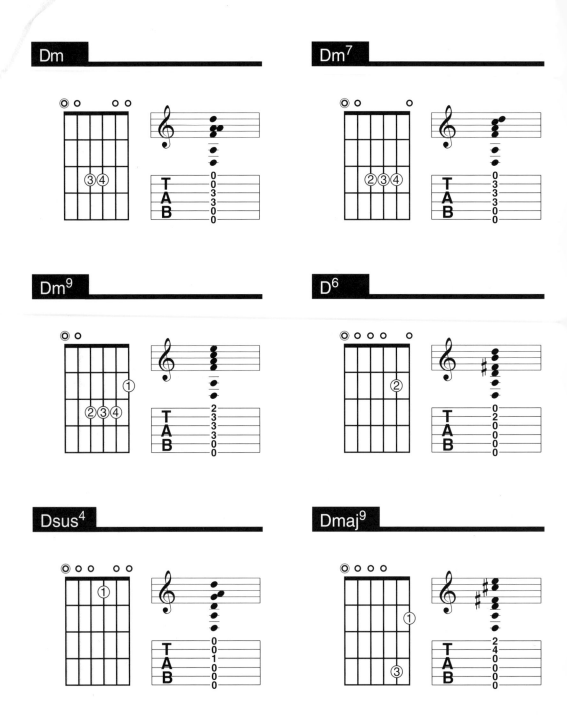

When your starting point is such a fantastic-sounding D chord, it doesn't take a lot of effort to come up with some good variations. Here are six of the simplest.

Further ideas

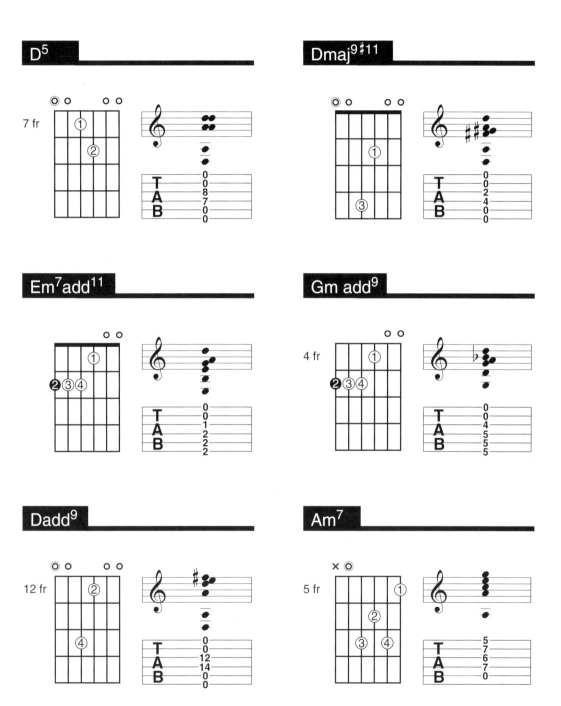

Despite the complex names, none of these chords is difficult. Two of these (Em7add11 and Gmadd9) use the common technique of moving a fretted shape around while keeping the first two strings open.

'Little Black Cab'

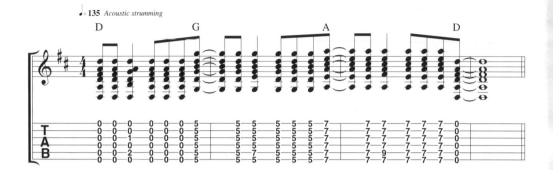

This acoustic rhythm part works equally well with or without a capo, and it's also possible to work out a version that doesn't use the open chord. It's based on one-finger six-string barre shapes, with extra fingers added and taken away to create new chords and rhythmic variations. Similar techniques are used in this tuning on Joni Mitchell's track *Big Yellow Taxi*.

'Delta Bad Card'

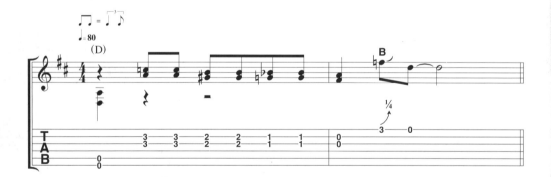

Open D tuning has also been used on early blues recordings by greats such as Son House, Elmore James and of course Robert Johnson. This descending outro line in the key of D is a typical example. Use all downstrokes with the plectrum, or play the double-stopped notes using two fingers at a time. Note the bluesy quarter-tone bend in the second bar.

Joni Mitchell never learned to play in normal tuning, but used over 50 of her own devising!

5

DADGAD Tuning

6	5	4	3	2	1
D	A	D	G	A	D
-2	0	0	0	-2	-2

The DADGAD tuning (pronounced 'Dad-Gad') is a curious beast – it sounds like it's been around for centuries, and is used to play many ancient folk tunes, and yet it was almost certainly invented by 1950s acoustic player Davey Graham. Since then, it's appeared on the acoustic recordings of Richard Thompson, Pierre Bensusan and Nick Harper, but never more famously than in the Led Zeppelin tracks *Black*

Mountain Side and *Kashmir*.

DADGAD, when strummed open, creates a chord of Dsus4. It isn't easy to get to grips with at first because it's not based on an open chord, and yet it is still altered very heavily from standard tuning, making new chord shapes difficult to play and to work out. However, once you've figured out even two or three basic shapes, the whole rune-clad Celtic world of magic and mystery is yours for the taking!

Tuning Guide

Starting from normal EADGBE tuning, drop the outer two strings to D as explained in previous chapters. Play the third string at the 2nd fret, then lower the tuning of the second string until the two are the same pitch. If your guitar has a particularly high action, you may find the harmonic method more accurate; play a 12th fret harmonic on the fifth string lower the 2nd string note until it matches. To check, fret the third string at the 2nd fret and strum all six.

Dsus⁴

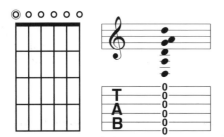

D

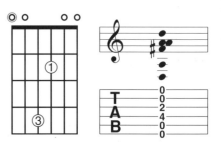

Basic chords

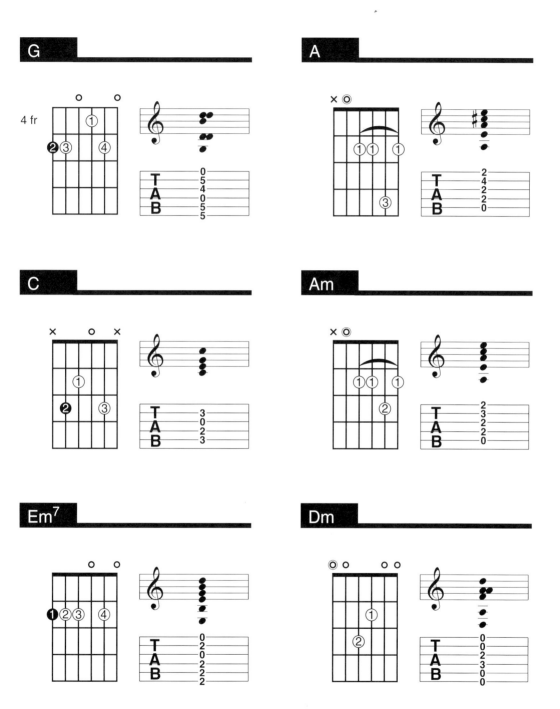

DADGAD isn't really designed for playing straight major and minor strummed chords, so don't worry if you find these chords more difficult than the ones with more obscure-sounding names.

D chords

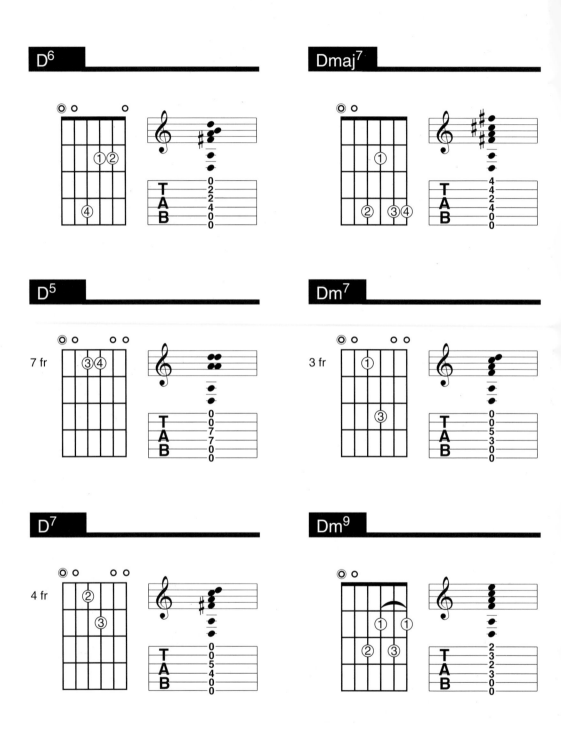

Despite the weird shapes, all of these chords are based in DADGAD's home key of D. Of these, the D5 is possibly the most useful because it has the open 'Gaelic' sound often associated with this tuning.

Further ideas

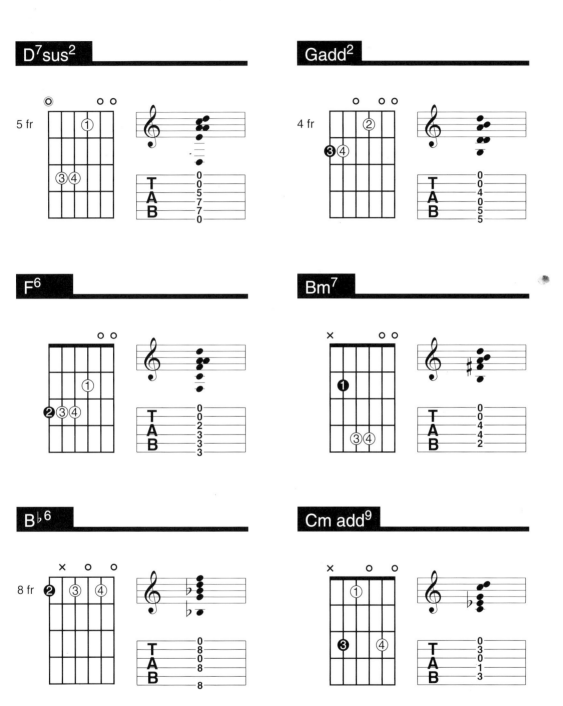

Note that because of the unusual tuning, some chords which you wouldn't normally associate with the key of D (e.g. Cmadd9, B♭6) fall fairly comfortably under the fingers.

'Maypole Dance'

Folk guitarists often use the open strings associated with DADGAD for this type of Celtic effect. Although it's based on a drone-line chord of D5, the rapidly-shifting melody implies chords of D7 and D. As with many folk-based styles, maximum use is made of the open strings as part of the melody, and hammer-ons and slides are used wherever possible.

'Wing And A Page'

Here's a DADGAD trick that I've been using for years. Learn this scale (it's actually the D Mixolydian mode, theory fans) on the third string as shown, then slide your hand up and down the neck, choosing any notes of the scale that you think sound good. Now do the same thing while strumming all six strings. Hey presto – instant Led Zeppelin!

Folk player Richard
Thompson went all Celtic
with his DADGAD tuning.

There are no rules about what makes a good alternate tuning – if it works for you, then use it! Acoustic players of the '60s and '70s (notably Stephen Stills and Nick Drake) often made up tunings on the spot to suit their needs, and some more electrified artists such as Soundgarden and Sonic Youth have brought the 'devised' tuning right up to date.

In this chapter is a selection of some of the less common tunings, together with some ideas for adapting them to your own style and sound. All of these have been used on guitar recordings during the last 30 years, but they're not as accessible or immediate as some of the others we've looked at. Some of the examples (Nashville tuning particularly) will need different string gauges on your guitar. So if you break a string, don't send me the bill!

Open E5

6	5	4	3	2	1
E	B	E	E	B	E
0	+2	+2	-3	0	0

This tuning, and its semitone-dropped brother open E♭5, has been used by Stephen Stills and The Gary Glitter band. Although it creates a 'power chord' played open, its unison E notes can be very effective as part of an acoustic fingerstyle accompaniment.

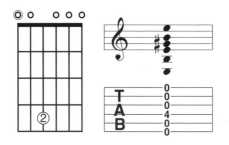

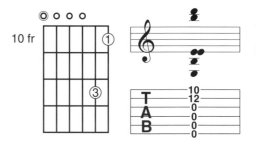

'Two Score And Nine'

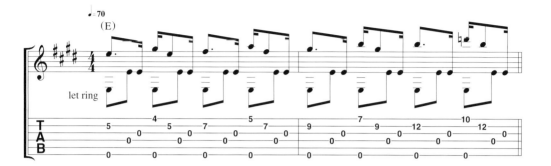

In this fingerpicked example, the thumb plays the sixth and fourth strings only (both tuned to E), but the first finger covers the third string (also E), creating an interesting doubled note in the almost sitar-like accompaniment. The second and third fingers of the picking hand articulate the melody, which is played in intervals of thirds on the first two strings.

'#12 Chorus'

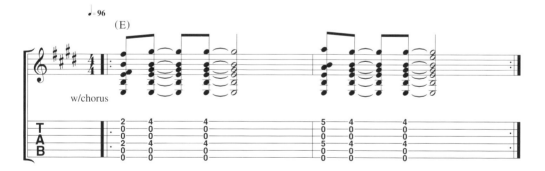

In this tuning, the in-built unisons and repeated octave notes imply a 12-string effect anyway, so it's a relatively simple matter to come up with finger shapes that make big, expansive acoustic chords. Both the fretted notes here are the same, albeit an octave apart. You might also like to try the same strings played up at the 7th, 9th, 10th, 11th and 12th frets.

This is one of the few photos of Nick Drake, who used open tunings extensively until his death at the age of 24.

Dropped Top D Tuning

6	5	4	3	2	1
E	A	D	G	B	D
0	0	0	0	0	-2

If you're only going to alter one string from regular tuning, it doesn't have to be in the bass end (for example, dropping the third string down to F# creates 'Lute' tuning, which many classical players still use).

This example simply lowers the first string by a tone – I call it 'lazy bottleneck' tuning because you can use it to play the majority of Open G slide lead licks (see page 23) without deviating too far from regular tuning when you're playing live. However, it also gives you the option of that ringing D note in any open chords you might come up with.

Cadd⁹

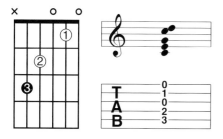

E⁷

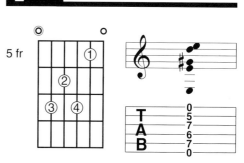

G

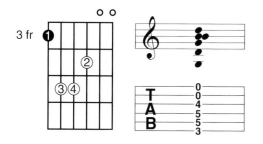

A

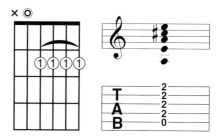

'All The Fourths' Tuning

6	5	4	3	2	1
E	A	D	G	C	F
0	0	0	0	+1	+1

Regular tuning is the most convenient and versatile compromise for the guitar (which is why we use it) but that doesn't necessarily make it the most logical. All orchestral stringed instruments (e.g. violin, 'cello, double bass) are tuned in fourths or fifths, rather than the combination of intervals that guitarists use.

'All The Fourths' uses the same interval between each string – so you put your finger on the fifth fret of *every* string when you're tuning the guitar to itself. It's not especially versatile, but many jazz players swear by it.

F

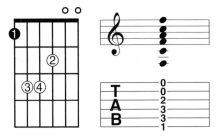

G⁷sus⁴

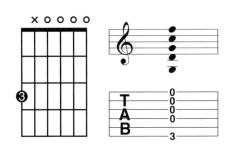

E

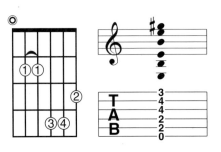

Dm⁷

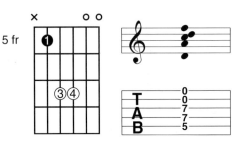

'New Clear Fusion'

Although this type of parallel-4ths double-stopped riff is normally associated with jazz or fusion, the example shown here should word just as well in a rock format. The tuning allows you to play what would normally be a fairly difficult lick at greater speed due to the fact that all the double-stops can use the same flattened finger shape.

'Scale With Harmonics'

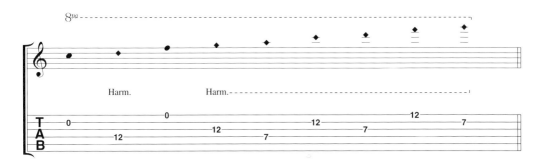

Every new tuning brings with it new opportunities for open harmonics, and this one is no exception. This is a scale of D minor pentatonic, played using a combination of open notes and open harmonics at the 12th and 7th frets. Play the scale as shown, then play it in reverse, making sure that all the open notes and harmonics ring on. The effect is very harp-like.

Nashville Tuning

6	5	4	3	2	1
E	A	D	G	B	E
+12	+12	+12	0	0	0

You can only really try this one out if you've got a spare guitar or a lot of patience, because it involves restringing every time you want to use it. Nashville tuning is identical to regular tuning except the three 'bass' strings are tuned an octave higher (suggested electric gauges .024-

.015-.012-.017-.013-.010). It creates a chiming, 'jangly' sound, and works equally well on electric and acoustic guitar. It's particularly easy to use because we already know all the chord shapes, but don't try to play straightforward solos unless you're prepared for some very strange results!

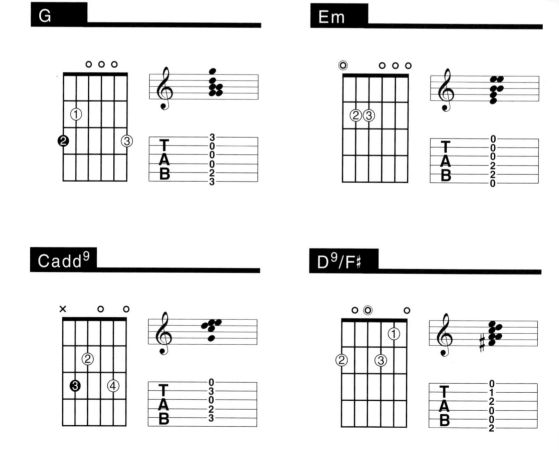

'Wrong Way Up'

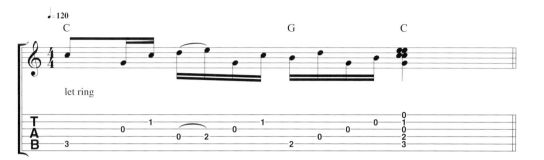

This flash-sounding country picking lick is much simpler than it seems. Check out the tab and you'll see ordinary chord shapes of C, G and C again, played fingerstyle using three fingers and the thumb. However, because of all the confused octaves Nashville tuning gives us, the effect is quite startling. As long as you can play it as fast as those Nashville cats...

'Chiming Scale'

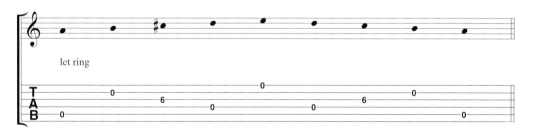

Nashville tuning has also recently been used by John Squire on Stone Roses' recordings, and this technique is a good example of the way electric players can use it in a more indie-rock context than its country name would suggest. Simply pick the strings shown while fretting the third string, and the resulting scale should give you loads of ideas for variations.

Jeff Buckley experimented with tunings in the 90s - just like his dad Tim in the 70s.

Hopefully the examples shown here should give you enough inspiration to devise some tunings of your own. Remember, there are no rules about what you can and can't do; as long as it sounds good, and your string gauge will cope with it, any tuning you devise is fair game. Listen to artists like Jeff Buckley and Bernard Butler to hear what can be achieved with imaginative use of tunings.

It's not worth spending a lot of time working out new fingerings for the familiar chords you normally use - you'll be wasting all of the creative potential of the tuning. Use altered tunings as they were meant to be used – to expand the range of sounds and textures you can produce from your guitar – and you'll be well on the way to becoming a better all-round musician.

Do...

- ...figure out whether your string gauge can cope with the tuning. If you're playing electric guitar fitted with .009 gauge strings, you won't get a particularly great sound out of Open C tuning, for example, unless you select a higher gauge.

- ...devise your own tunings. Try starting with one from this book, then altering one note to see what results it produces – e.g. if you start in Open D tuning and drop the third string down a half step (semitone) you get open D minor.

- ...make sure you're exactly *in tune*. Often a tuning might sound terrible simply because the notes aren't completely accurate. Check and double check, using a tuner if you have one.

- ...try using fingerstyle. By far the most frequent users of altered tunings are acoustic players, so if you've used a plectrum all your life, now's a great time to become a picker!

- ...try using bottleneck. You'll probably find that the open chord version work better for straight blues chords licks, but all of the tunings in the book have the *potential* for slide.

- ...experiment with capos. If you put the guitar in open D tuning, put a capo at the 4th fret and you've got instant open F# tuning.

- ...drop me a cyber-line! joe.bennett@ndirect.co.uk

Don't...

- ...tune up too far! If you're raising any note by more than a whole step (two frets' worth) you're substantially increasing the risk of string breakage. If in doubt, figure out the whole tuning a step lower, and use a capo.

- ...be put off if the tuning doesn't sound good when all the notes are played open. Not all 'altered' tunings have to create a chord on their own. Maybe you just have to find the right fingering to get the best out of it.

- ...rely too much on your usual techniques. For example, if bends work well on the third string in regular tuning, perhaps the altered version might be more flattering to another string?

- ...strum every chord you see in this book. Some of the chord shapes work better played fingerstyle, and some may be more effective when picked one note at a time.

- ...give up too soon on a tuning. It might have taken many years to get to your current level in regular tuning, so be prepared to put in the hours before you hear something really good.

- ...try all the examples in the book on the same instrument. Some of them work better on acoustic, some on electric, some both.

- ...forget which tuning you're using half-way through a song. Very embarrassing indeed!

Other Books of Interest

The Nick Drake Song Collection
A unique collection of his finest songs in full piano, voice and guitar arrangements, complete with guitar chord boxes, original guitar tunings and full lyrics. Includes fully illustrated lyrics section with rare archive photographs and preface by Robert Kirby.
Order No.AM92388

John Martyn for Guitar Tab
A collection of ten songs reflecting the inspiring musicianship of John Martyn, a unique singer-songwriter and skilled guitarist whose career spans more than 25 years. In tablature and standard notation, with chord symbols, melody line and lyrics.
Order No.AM91531

Bernard Butler: People Move On
All the songs from the album in complete guitar tablature and standard notation arrangements. Includes section of lyrics and full details of alternate tunings.
Order No.AM953766

These, and many more, superb music books are available from your local music dealer or, in case of difficulty, direct from Music Sales Limited, Newmarket Road, Bury St. Edmunds, Suffolk IP33 3YB.